Super-Duper Series

The Wheels on the Bus

by Annalisa McMorrow
illustrated by Marilynn G. Barr

Publisher: Roberta Suid
Design & Production: Scott McMorrow
Educational Consultant: Shirley Ross
Cover Design: David Hale
Cover Art: Mike Artell

Also in this series:
Ladybug, Ladybug (MM 2015), *Twinkle, Twinkle* (MM 2016),
Rub-a-Dub-Dub (MM 2017), *Pussycat, Pussycat* (MM 2036),
Daffy-Down-Dilly (MM 2037), *Rain, Rain, Go Away!* (MM 2038),
Snips & Snails (MM 2096), *Sticks & Stones* (MM 2097),
A Diller, A Dollar (MM 2099)

Contents

Introduction

The Wheels on the Bus is composed of five chapters, each a complete unit dedicated to a specific type of vehicle. This resource has a cross-curricular approach that helps children develop a hands-on understanding of transportation while strengthening language skills, such as speaking and listening. Children will relate to cars, bicycles, buses, planes, and trains in a personal way: learning through games, observations, literature links, math activities, songs, and art.

Let's Read features a popular children's book, such as *Curious George Rides a Bike* by H.A. Rey, and is accompanied by a detailed plot description. **Let's Talk** helps children link the featured book with familiar feelings, thoughts, or happenings in their own lives. For example, in the Cars chapter, the "Let's Talk" discussion focuses on a time when children took a ride in an automobile. This page also includes a pattern that can be duplicated and used as a bookmark.

Let's Learn is filled with facts about each vehicle. For example, early bicycles had giant front wheels and very small rear wheels. Choose facts that you think will interest the children. Read a fact a day during the unit. Or write down different facts and post them around the room.

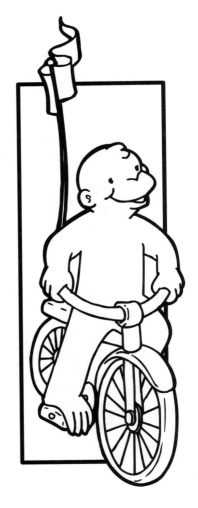

The **Let's Create** activities in each chapter allow children to use their imaginations while honing small motor skills. The children will make their own shoe box buses, Cinderella carriages, and much more.

Children make a hands-on learning connection in the **Let's Find Out** activities. These projects focus on exploration, leading children through moments of discovery as they graph vehicles, find out about bicycle safety, learn foreign words for different vehicles, and much more.

Let's Play suggests a new game to interest children in the topic of the moment. **Let's Eat** offers suggestions for snacks that tie into the chapter's theme. A song sung to a familiar tune is featured in the **Let's Sing** section. Children can learn the new lyrics and perform them for parents or each other. Duplicate the songs and send them home with the children to share with their families.

Informative Pattern Pages complete each chapter. These patterns can be duplicated and used for bulletin board displays, reduced for cubby labels or name tags, or used for desk labeling. (Children can color the patterns using crayons or markers.)

At the end of the book, you'll find a Storybook Resources section filled with additional fiction picture books and storybooks, plus a Nonfiction Resources section suggesting factual and photographic books of the featured vehicles.

All About Planes, Trains, Automobiles, and More...

Wheels are important to most forms of transportation. Cars, bicycles, buses, trains, and planes all have wheels. However, nobody knows who invented the wheel or when the wheel was invented. Vehicles with wheels have been used for at least 5,000 years.

Before there were cars or trucks, horses and oxen pulled carriages. This is why people still talk about a car or truck's "horsepower."

When children are on car trips, they may notice the many different types of cars on the road. Some are old, with designs very different from modern cars. Old cars have designs that we no longer consider modern, such as tail fins. Some new cars are designed to look like old cars—the new VW bug, for example. People who design cars try out their ideas on computers. They work to make cars safer and more efficient. In the car chapter, children will design their own cars.

My car can fly when the sun is up.

During this unit, consider taking the children on a field trip to ride a train, bus, trolley, cable car, or ferry. Or take the children to a car or airplane museum or a car show. This unit is also a good time to discuss vehicle safety. Remind children to always wear seat belts when they are passengers and to wear helmets when they ride their bicycles.

Cars

Introduction

• Let's Read:
Mr. Grumpy's Motor Car by John Burningham (HarperCollins, 1973).
On a beautiful day, Mr. Grumpy takes an assortment of children and animals on a ride through the countryside. When the weather changes, the children and animals must work together to push the car out of the mud. All return happily for a clean-up swim at home.

• Let's Talk:
Most of the time, people drive cars to get from one place to another. Discuss a time when the children went with their families or friends on a ride just for the fun of a ride. This book also offers the opportunity to discuss cooperation. Although nobody really wants to get out and push the car from the mud puddle, it takes the whole team working together to get the car unstuck! The children can share a time when they cooperated to get a job done.

• Let's Learn:
Before there were cars, people rode in horse-drawn wagons and carriages. The inventors of automobiles had to invent a carriage that would turn its own wheels. In the first cars, the driver had to turn a handle on the front of a car to get it started. Now, all drivers have to do is turn a key. Today's cars have many safety features that were missing from horse-drawn carriages. These include headlights, taillights, windshield wipers, and horns. Cars continue to change. In the future, cars may be run by solar power or on electric batteries.

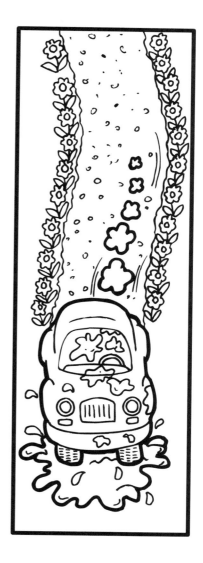

Book Link:
• *Cars and How They Go* by Joanna Cole, illustrated by Gail Gibbons (Crowell, 1983).
This is a great book for a more in-depth look at how cars work.

Cars

Let's Create: An Auto Parade

Mr. Grumpy takes a whole group of people and animals on a ride. Ask the children who they would like to take on a ride in their cars.

What You Need:
Cool Cars (p. 9), crayons or markers, glitter mixed with glue (in squeeze bottles), tag board, scissors

What You Do:
1. Duplicate the Cool Cars onto tag board and cut them out. Make one for each child.
2. Provide crayons and markers for the children to use to decorate their cars. The children can also use the glitter-glue mixture to add extra sparkle.
3. Have the children draw pictures of their friends, pets, and family in the backs of the cars.
4. Post the completed cars on an "Auto Parade" bulletin board.

Option:
• Ask the parents to send in photos of their children that can be used in an arts-and-crafts activity. Let the children cut their faces from the photos and glue them in the driver's seats of their cars.

Book Link:
• *Cars! Cars! Cars!* by Grace Maccarone, illustrated by David A. Carter (Scholastic, 1995).
This adorable, colorful book features different types of cars.

Cool Cars

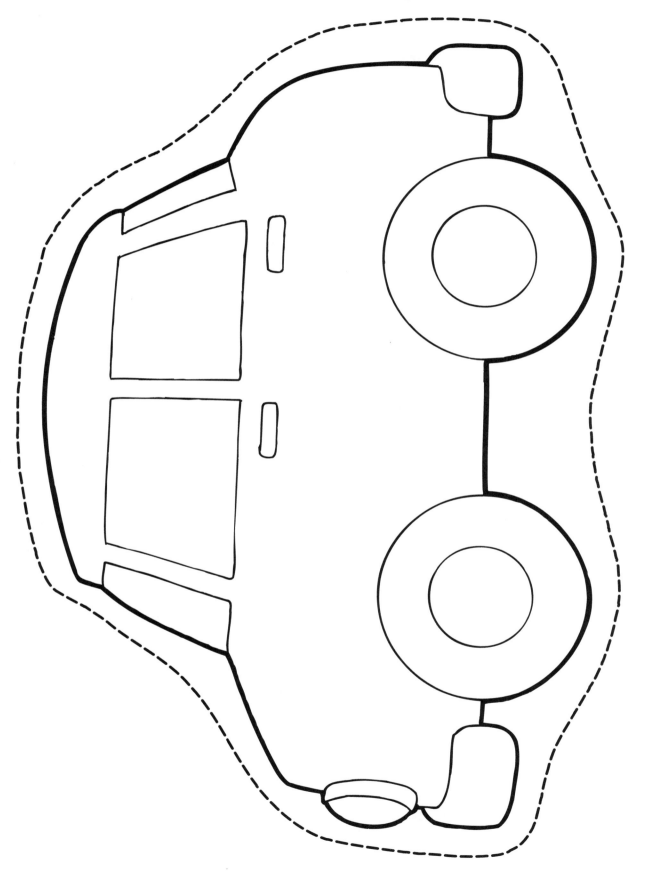

Cars

Let's Create: A Cabbage Carriage

What You Need:
Assorted round or oval fruits and vegetables (apple, orange, grape, tomato, potato, cabbage), paper, crayons and markers, glitter mixed with glue (in squeeze bottles)

What You Do:
1. Read or tell the story of Cinderella.
2. Have the children imagine a pumpkin turned into a carriage.
3. Display the fruits and vegetables for the children to observe.
4. Have the children imagine that instead of a pumpkin, Cinderella's fairy godmother used a different vegetable or fruit for the carriage.
5. Have the children draw their own versions of Cinderella's carriage, using a fruit or vegetable other than a pumpkin as the starting point.
6. Post the completed pictures on a "Caravan of Carriages" bulletin board.

Option:
• In the fall, purchase a small pumpkin. Using plastic horses, set up a Cinderella's Carriage display in the classroom.

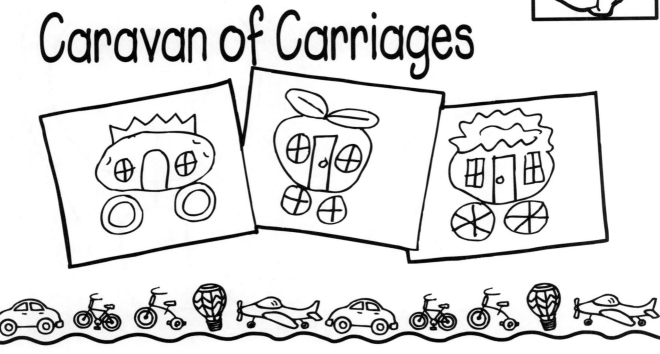

Caravan of Carriages

Cars

Let's Create: Amazing Automobiles

Since the invention of the car, people have created many different unusual vehicles. The German Amphicar (created in the 1960s) could travel on water or land. The Aerocar was a flying car made to avoid traffic jams. A fruit company created "mobile oranges" that were round, fruit-shaped automobiles.

What You Need:
Small milk cartons or empty tissue boxes, construction paper, scissors, glue, crayons or markers, spools, fabric scraps, pipe cleaners, additional craft materials

What You Do:
1. Describe some of the amazing automobiles that inventors have created in the past.
2. Explain that the children will be making their own amazing autos. They should imagine what they would want a car to be able to do—travel on water, fly, come when they called it, drive on command without a driver, and so on.
3. Provide clean, empty milk cartons or empty tissue boxes and an assortment of craft materials for the children to use to make their own amazing automobiles.
4. When the creations have dried, let the children share their automobiles with the class, explaining the features that make their cars special.

Cars

Let's Create: Cardboard Cars

What You Need:
Cardboard boxes (one per child; the boxes should be large enough to fit around a child's waist), tempera paint, paintbrushes, shallow tins (for paint), ice pick (for punching holes in cardboard; for adult use only), thick yarn, scissors, craft knife (for adult use only)

What You Do:
1. Cut the bottom and top off of each box. Punch four holes in each box, two in the front and two in the rear. The holes should line up.
2. Give one box to each child.
3. Have the children paint their boxes to resemble cars. They can paint the boxes any color they wish. The children may want to paint on headlights, taillights, doors, and license plates.
4. When the cardboard cars are dry, string a piece of yarn through each set of two holes on the boxes. (The cars will be worn like sandwich boards, with the yarn over the children's shoulders.)
5. Let the children use their cars in dramatic play.

Option:
• Discuss traffic safety while the children are in their cars. Go over what the different traffic lights and traffic signs represent.

Cars

Let's Create: Driver's License

This activity reinforces the children's knowledge of where they live and how to write their names.

What You Need:
Driver's Licenses (p. 14), crayons or markers, scissors, clear contact paper or laminating machine, photos of the children and glue (optional)

What You Do:
1. Duplicate a copy of the Driver's License for each child and cut them out.
2. Have the children either glue their photos or draw self-portraits in the rectangles.
3. Let the children dictate their addresses. Write these down in the appropriate places.
4. Have the children print their names on their licenses. Help those who need it.
5. Laminate the completed licenses. Or cover them with clear contact paper.
6. Let the children use their licenses in dramatic play with their Cardboard Cars.

Option:
• Use these driver's licenses as desk or cubby labels for Open House. Parents will be able to identify their child's area.

Driver's Licenses

Cars

Let's Find Out: Traffic Jam Graph

What You Need:
Vehicle Patterns (p. 16), large sheet of paper, crayons or markers, scissors, tape

What You Do:
1. Duplicate the Vehicle Patterns and cut them out. Make one extra set for teacher use.
2. Let each child choose his or her favorite vehicle.
3. Provide crayons and markers for the children to use to decorate their vehicles. Help the children write their names on their vehicles.
4. Make a six-columned graph. At the top, write "Which Is Your Favorite?" Glue one of the Vehicle Patterns above each column.
5. Mix all of the vehicles together in a traffic jam pile.
6. One by one, pick a vehicle from the traffic jam, and read aloud whose vehicle it is. Let the child come up and tape it into the correct column.
7. When all of the choices have been recorded, discuss the finished graph together. Begin the discussion by asking the children what they notice about the graph.

Option:
Have the children cut pictures of vehicles from old magazines. Use these pictures to make a graph.

Book Link:
• *Traffic: A Book of Opposites* by Betsy and Giulio Maestro (Crown, 1981).
This colorful book uses traffic situations to teach opposites.

Vehicle Patterns

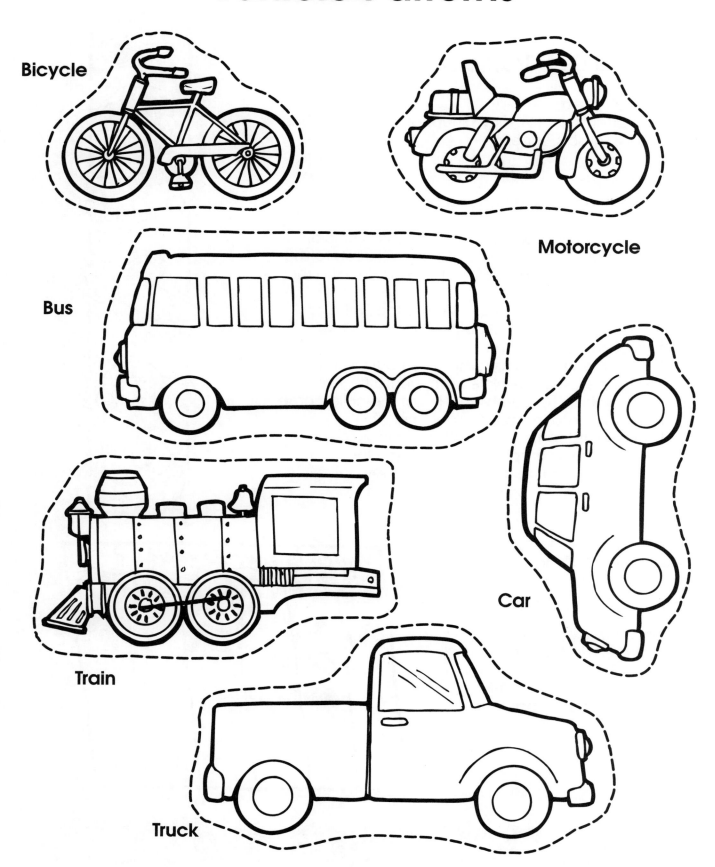

Bicycle

Motorcycle

Bus

Car

Train

Truck

Cars

Let's Find Out: In Other Words

What You Need:
Pictures of vehicles, drawing paper, crayons or markers

What You Do:
1. Explain to the children that different languages have different words for vehicles. For example, in German, the word for car is "Auto." In Italian, the word for car is "macchina." In French, a car is a "voiture." In Spanish, the word for car is "coche." Even in English, we have many different words for the objects that we drive.
2. Have the children name as many vehicles (or things that help people go places) as possible. These might include automobile (or auto), bus, car, SUV, station wagon, truck, motorcycle, and vehicle.
3. Show the children pictures of different vehicles. (Use the vehicle patterns or pictures from books or magazines.) Have them brainstorm words that describe the different vehicles.
4. Give each child a piece of paper.
5. Have the children draw pictures of vehicles.
6. Let each child have a turn dictating a word or a descriptive phrase for his or her vehicle.
7. Post the finished pictures on a bulletin board that lists the different foreign words for cars.

Note:
If any of the children in your class speak other languages, have them share their country's word for car.

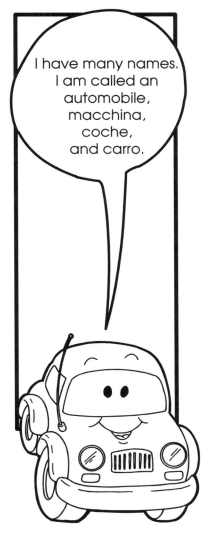

Cars

Let's Find Out: What Lights Mean

What You Need:
One large milk carton, small milk cartons (one for each child), colored construction paper (red, yellow, green), glue, scissors

What You Do:
1. Make a traffic light by cutting out red, yellow, and green construction paper circles and gluing them in the correct order to the milk carton.
2. Hold the carton up in the classroom. Explain that it represents a traffic light.
3. One at a time, point to each of the different colors, and have the children tell what the color means. (Red = stop, yellow = slow down, and green = go.)
4. Cut enough colored circles for each child to have one of each color.
5. Give each child a small, clean milk carton and three colored construction paper circles.
6. Have the children make their own traffic lights by gluing the colored circles on in the correct order.
7. Punch a hole in the top of each milk carton and thread through with a piece of yarn. The children can take home their traffic lights to hang in their rooms.

Cars

Let's Find Out: Traffic Sign Symbols

What You Need:
Signs (p. 20), scissors, crayons or markers, craft sticks, glue, clay

What You Do:
1. Duplicate the signs and cut them out. Make enough for each child to have a set.
2. Have the children look at the signs. Then ask them what they think the different signs mean.
3. Go over the correct answers: The stop sign means stop. The R/R sign designates a railroad crossing. The sign with the numbers tells a driver the speed limit (how fast he or she can drive). The yield sign means that a driver must let other cars have the right of way. One way means that cars on this road all travel in the direction the arrow is pointing.
4. Have the children color the signs.
5. The children can glue craft sticks to the backs of the signs, and then stick the free ends of the sticks in small balls of clay for bases.
6. These signs can be used in play with the children's Amazing Automobiles (p. 11).

Cars

Let's Play: Red Light, Green Light

What You Need:
Nothing

What You Do:
Explain the rules of the game to the students. One child is the traffic light. All of the other children line up in a row facing the traffic light. They should be about 30 feet (10 m) away from the "light." The child playing the traffic light turns his or her back on the other children and says "green light." All of the other children move forward until the child says "red light" and turns around to face them. No one can move when the traffic light is facing them. The game continues, switching from red light to green light until one of the other children is able to tag the "traffic light." That child becomes the next "traffic light."

Red light!

Cars

Let's Eat: Fast Food

Let the children eat their snacks while wearing their Cardboard Cars (p. 12).

What You Need:
Easy-to-eat snacks, such as carrot sticks, celery sticks, pretzels, or crackers

What You Do:
1. Discuss the concept of fast-food restaurants. People are able to drive up to a window and order their food. They can then take their food home or eat the food in their cars.
2. Set up a drive-through window. This can simply be a table with the snacks set up in a row.
3. Have the children put on their Cardboard Cars and line up at the drive-through window.
4. Give each child a snack to eat while in his or her car.

Cars

Let's Sing: Driving Songs

I'm a Car
(to the tune of "This Old Man")

I'm a car.
I'm a car.
Get inside, and we'll drive far,
With a put-put, vroom-vroom-vroom,
Chugga-chugg-all day.
This small car will drive away.

A Green Light Means "Go"
(to the tune of "Do Your Ears Hang Low?")

A green light means "go,"
And a yellow means "go slow."
If you drive up to a red,
Then you'll have to stop instead.
When you find a red stop sign,
Stop behind the thick, white line.
A green light means "go."

When I'm Driving
(to the tune of "Clementine")

When I'm driving,
When I'm driving,
And I come to a stop sign,
Then I stop and I look both ways
And I stay behind the line.

With a put-put, vroom-vroom-vroom. Chugga-chugg-all day. This small car will drive away.

"I'm a Car!"

Buses

Introduction

• Let's Read:
This Is the Way We Go to School: A Book About Children Around the World by Edith Baer, illustrated by Steve Bjorkman (Scholastic, 1990).

Many children take a school bus to school. However, there are lots of ways that children around the world get to school. Some children walk slowly to school, others jog, and others roller skate. In San Francisco, some children take cable cars to school. In Venice, some children ride the vaporetto!

• Let's Talk:
Have the children share the ways they go to school. If children don't ride the school bus, ask if any of the children have ever ridden on any type of bus. Let the children discuss different bus rides they may have taken. Then discuss ways that other children around the world get to school.

    This is also a perfect time to discuss your school's rules for riding the school bus. Consider inviting a school bus driver to discuss the rules with the children.

• Let's Learn:
There are many different types of buses the children may have ridden on or seen—school buses, city buses, extra-long buses (the size of two regular city buses hinged together at the middle), double-decker buses, tour buses (with convertible tops). But the children may be unaware that the very first buses, which started service in Paris in 1662, were actually pulled by horses!

Buses

Let's Create: The Children on the Bus

What You Need:
Large sheet of butcher paper, yellow tempera paint, paintbrushes, shallow tins (for paint), construction paper in people colors, crayons or markers, glue, black marker

What You Do:
1. Draw a large bus on the butcher paper.
2. Let the children paint the bus yellow.
3. Cut the people-colored construction paper into circles the size of small paper plates. Let the children choose the color of paper they want to use for their self-portraits.
4. Have the children draw their faces on the circles.
5. Once the bus is dry, glue the circles to the windows in the bus. The children can help choose where they'd like to be in the bus.
6. Post the bus mural in the classroom or in the library. Put a display of books about buses on a table below the mural.

Bus Book:
• *Wheels on the Bus* illustrated by Sylvie Kantorovitz Wickstrom (Crown, 1990).
In Raffi's songs-to-read series, this book gives many different verses of the famous song.

Option:
• Make a smaller bus and let the children glue photographs of themselves in the bus's windows.

Buses

Let's Create: Double-Decker Buses

Different areas in the world have different types of transportation.

What You Need:
Shoe boxes (two per child, or two per team), red tempera paint, paintbrushes, shallow tins (for paint), glue or tape, black construction paper, scissors, blocks, plastic people and cars

What You Do:
1. Explain that some buses have an upstairs and a downstairs. In London, the double-decker buses on the streets are colored bright red.
2. Divide children into teams of two, or let each child work alone. Give each child or team two shoe boxes to paint red.
3. Once the paint has dried, the children can cut out black construction paper wheels to glue to one of their boxes.
4. When the wheels have dried, the children can glue or tape one shoe box on top of the other. (The one with the wheels should be on the bottom.)
5. The children can create cities with blocks and plastic cars and people. Their double-decker buses can drive through these cities.

Option:
• Some children may want to make single-decker school buses. Provide yellow paint for this activity.

Buses

Let's Find Out: "B" Words

What You Need:
"I'm a Bus!" pattern (p. 34), crayons or markers, chalk, hole punch, brads or yarn

What You Do:
1. Duplicate a copy of the "I'm a Bus!" pattern for each child.
2. Write the word "bus" on the board. Go over each of the letters that makes up the word bus. Ask the children which letter "bus" starts with.
3. Have the children brainstorm other words that start with the letter "b." Write their words on the board. For a list of words that start with "b," see below.
4. Have each child illustrate one word that starts with "b" on the "I'm a Bus!" pattern. The children can illustrate more than one word if they want.
5. The children should either write the words they've chosen on their pages, or dictate the words to be written down for them.
6. Collect the completed pages and punch holes on one side. Bind the pages together in a classroom "Starts with B" book. Consider creating letter books for all of the alphabet.

"B" Words for Children to Illustrate:
Baby, backpack, ball, balloon, banana, band, bandage, basket, bat, bean, bear, bee, beet, bib, bike, binder, bird, biscuit, boat, book, bride, bridge, bubble, bull

Buses

Let's Find Out: Counting Wheels

What You Need:
"I'm a Bus!" pattern (p. 34), Wheel Patterns (p. 30), crayons or markers, scissors

What You Do:
1. Duplicate a copy of the Bus Pattern and the Wheel Patterns for each child.
2. Provide crayons or markers for the children to use to color their buses.
3. Have the children cut out the wheels.
4. Lead the children through simple counting activities. For example, have the children start by placing four wheels on the bus. Then have them add two more. Ask the children how many wheels there are now. (They can count the wheels to find the answer.) Then have the children take off four wheels. Ask how many wheels there are now.
5. When you are done with the different math problems, the children can glue the wheels to the buses.

Wheel Patterns

Buses

Let's Play: Ride the Bus

This is a fun, dramatic play activity. Most children love pretending to go on a trip!

What You Need:
Small chairs, one larger chair

What You Do:
1. Set up a make-believe bus in the classroom. Simply line chairs in two long rows. Put a larger chair for the driver at the front of one of the rows.
2. The children can be passengers while you "drive" them on an imaginary journey. Describe the sights that they will be seeing out the windows. (Choose a journey ahead of time, or let the children suggest one.)
3. After one or more teacher-driven rides, let the children take turns pretending to be the driver.

Option:
• Create colorful paper tickets that the children can give the driver when they first get on the bus.

Book Link:
• *School Bus* by Donald Crews (Puffin, 1985).
Introduce this activity with this easy-to-read book.

Buses

Let's Eat: Yummy Yellow Foods

What You Need:
Lemon-flavored Jell-O, bananas, yellow summer squash, corn, apple juice, yellow apples

What You Do:
1. Have the children name the color of a school bus. (If your school bus isn't yellow, try to find foods that are the color of the bus.)
2. Have the children think of foods that are the same color as the bus.
3. Serve yellow snacks for the children to try. If you serve summer squash, cut it into sticks and offer it with a vegetable dip.

Mmmm!
Yellow squash.

Buses

Let's Sing: Bus Songs

"I'm a School Bus"
(to the tune of "Alouette")

I'm a school bus,
Yes, I am a school bus.
I'm a school bus.
I drive kids to school.
I'm a big, bright yellow bus.
I drive kids without a fuss.
Yellow bus,
Yellow bus,
There's no fuss,
There's no fuss.
Ohhhh,
I'm a school bus,
Yes, I am a school bus.
I'm a school bus.
I drive kids to school.

I Drive a Yellow School Bus
(to the tune of "Rudolph, the Red-Nosed Reindeer")

I drive a yellow school bus.
I pick children up at ten,
And when the day is over,
I bring them back home again.

CONE ELEMENTARY

I'm a a big bright yellow bus.
I drive kids without a fuss.
Yellow bus,
Yellow bus,
There's no fuss,
There's no fuss.

SCHOOL BUS

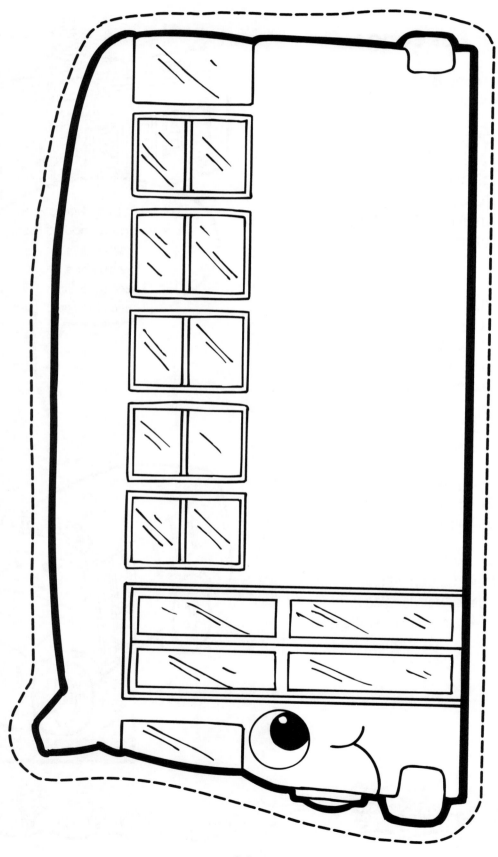

Trains

Introduction

• Let's Read:
The Little Engine That Could by Watty Piper (Platt & Munk, 1930). A little engine carrying toys and food for the children on the other side of the mountain breaks down. Its toy and doll cargo asks other engines for help to no avail. Finally, a little blue engine stops to help. Although it's not a big or fancy engine, it has the positive "I think I can" spirit needed to chug to the other side of the mountain. The 60th anniversary edition of this classic story was published in 1990.

• Let's Talk:
Have the children think about a time when they had to work hard to complete a task or to master a new activity—just like the little engine that could. For example, the children may have had to practice a lot before being able to ride a bike without training wheels, tie their shoes, make their beds, set the table, and so on. Let each child share a time when he or she had to behave like the Little Engine and think positive thoughts to get a job done.

This is a perfect time to talk about train safety, train signals, and staying away from train tracks.

• Let's Learn:
There are different types of trains. Freight trains carry objects and passenger trains carry people. Some trains travel underground. These trains are called subways or metros. Trains that travel above the streets are called elevated trains. Trains travel along tracks. Most trains travel on two tracks, but monorails travel on single tracks. The name for the person who drives a train is an engineer.

Trains

Let's Create: "I Think I Can" Train

What You Need:
"I'm a Train!" (p. 47), Train Car (p. 37), crayons or markers

What You Do:
1. Duplicate a copy of the Train Car for each child.
2. Have the children remember a time when they used positive thinking to finish a job or master a new skill.
3. Have the children draw a picture showing their positive thinking experience on the Train Cars.
4. Write "I Think I Can" on the "I'm a Train!" pattern. Post it at the start of a bulletin board, and post the children's pictures in a row behind it.

Options:
• Place books about trains on a desk or table below the "I Think I Can" train.
• Have the children draw pictures of things that they want to be able to do in the future: read, write, ride a two-wheeler, drive a car, cook, and so on.

Train Car

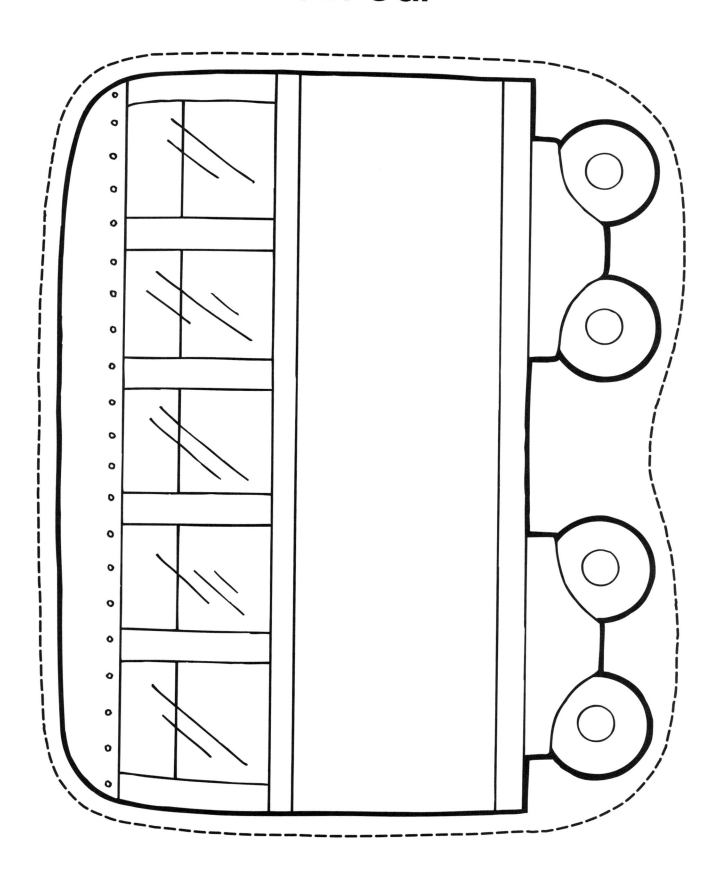

Trains

Let's Create: Toothpick Train Set

What You Need:
Toothpick boxes or other small boxes (one per child), craft sticks, construction paper, scissors, glue, marker

What You Do:
1. Give each child a small box.
2. Explain that the children will be making trains from their boxes. Provide construction paper scraps and glue for the children to use to decorate the little boxes.
3. Have the children create train tracks using the craft sticks. They can line the sticks up on the floor or glue them together.
4. When the trains are dry, write each child's name on his or her box. (Some children will be able to do this themselves.)
5. The children can scoot the trains along the tracks.

Options:
• If the children use more than one box, they can link the boxes together by punching holes in the ends and tying them together with yarn.
• Add posterboard wheels with brads.
• Use tissue boxes in place of toothpick boxes for larger trains.
• Use boxes of any size if toothpick boxes are too difficult to collect. Each child could bring several small boxes from home.

Trains

Let's Find Out: When the Train Leaves

The children will enjoy wearing these watches the old-fashioned way.

What You Need:
Watch Patterns (p. 40), tag board, crayons or markers, brads, scissors, hole punch, yarn

What You Do:
1. Duplicate the Watch Patterns and cut them out. Make enough for each child to have one. Cut out enough watch hands for each child to have a long one and a short one.
2. Cut the tag board into circles that are slightly larger than the watch faces.
3. Have the children glue the watch faces onto the circles.
4. Punch a hole in the center of each watch face, in each watch hand, and in the top of each watch fob.
5. Demonstrate how to attach two watch hands to the face of each watch with a brad. (The brad should close on the backside of the watch.)
6. Have the children thread a piece of yarn through the hole at the top of the watch. (To make pocket watches, they can attach the watches to their belt loops using the yarn.)
7. Practice telling time with the children. Have the children move the watch hands to different times that you call out. Walk around the class to make sure each child has the watch on the correct time. Then let the children use the watches to play "train conductor" and tell the engineer when it is time to start.

Book Link:
• *Choo Choo: The Story of a Little Engine Who Ran Away* by Virginia Lee Burton (Houghton Mifflin, 1937).
If possible, read this book before making the watches so that the children can see Archibald, the conductor, checking his pocket watch.

Watch Patterns

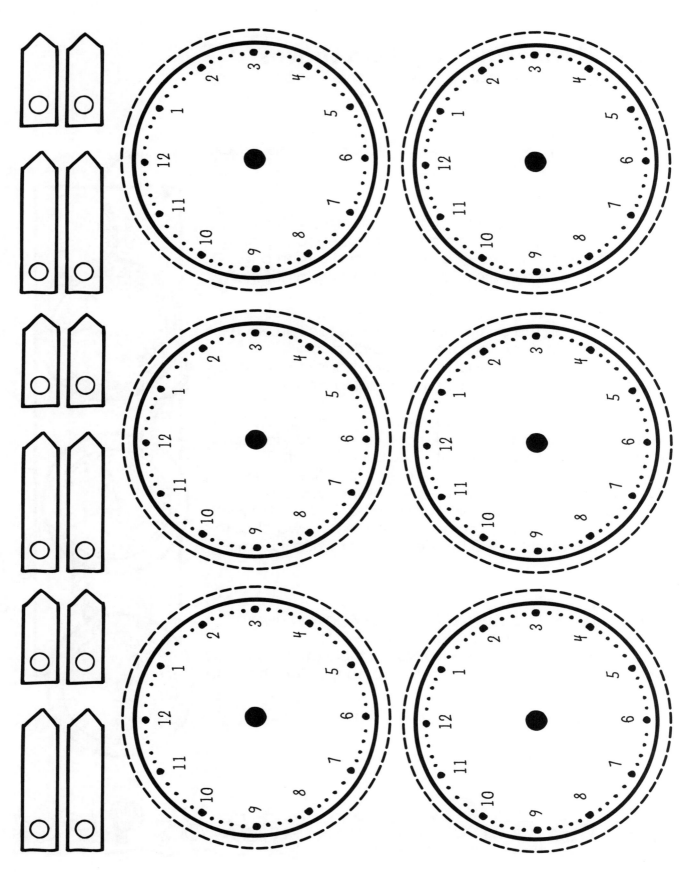

Trains

Let's Find Out: Alphabet Train Ride

Children will brainstorm objects and items that start with each letter of the alphabet.

What You Need:

Train Car (p. 37), crayons or markers

What You Do:

1. Make 26 copies of the Train Car.
2. Write one letter of the alphabet on each Train Car.
3. Have the children work together to brainstorm objects that start with each letter of the alphabet.
4. Give each child a Train Car and have the children illustrate one object that starts with the given alphabet letter. (Or let the children choose which letters they want to work on.) More than one child can add a picture to each car. Difficult letters can be left blank or illustrated by the teacher.
5. Post the completed alphabet train in correct ABC order on a wall of the classroom. Or bind the pages together in an Alphabet Train book.

Easy-to-Draw Objects for Each Letter:

Ant, banana, car, dog, egg, flower, grapes, hat, ice cream cone, jump rope, king, lion, man, nut, ocean, pipe, queen, rat, snake, turtle, umbrella, van, wall, x-ray, yak, zebra

Trains

Let's Play: Train, Train, Caboose
This game is played like "Duck, Duck, Goose."

What You Do:
1. Have the children sit in a circle.
2. Choose one child to be the "caboose."
3. This child walks around the circle, touching each of the other children gently on the head, and saying, "Train, train, train, train, train, train...caboose."
4. The tapped "caboose" chases the first caboose around the circle. If the tapper can sit in the vacated spot before being tagged, then the chaser is the new "caboose." Otherwise, the tapper must go to the center of the circle. This is called the "train yard."
5. Play continues with the new "caboose."

Option:
• The rest of the children can make train noises (whoo-whoo) while the cabooses chase each other around the circle.

Caboose!

Trains

Let's Play: Train-Centration

This game is played like "Concentration."

What You Need:

Train-Centration Cards (p. 44), markers or crayons, scissors, clear contact paper or laminator (optional)

What You Do:

1. Make two copies of the Train-Centration cards, color them, and cut them apart. Laminate or cover with clear contact paper, if desired. Cut out again leaving a thin laminate border to prevent peeling.

2. Demonstrate how to play "Train-Centration." The children turn all the cards face down. The first child turns two cards over at a time. If the cards match, the child keeps them and takes another turn. If the cards do not match, the child turns them back over and another child takes a turn.

Train-Centration Cards

Train Engine

Train Tracks

Freight Car

Passenger

Passenger Car

Caboose

Engineer

Luggage

Railroad Crossing Sign

44

Trains

Let's Eat: Carrot Railroad Cars

What You Need:
Carrot sticks, celery sticks, cream cheese, cucumber slices, thin pretzel sticks

What You Do:
1. Cut the carrot sticks into small, rectangular pieces.
2. Fill the celery sticks with cream cheese and cut them into small, rectangular pieces.
3. Cut the cucumbers into circles, then cut the circles in half.
4. The children can make trains by lining up carrot passenger cars, and celery stick freight cars. The cucumber slices can act as wheels, stuck to the trains with extra cream cheese.
5. Pretzel sticks can be the tracks for the trains to ride on, before they are eaten.

Book Link:
• *Trains* by Anne Rockwell (Dutton, 1988).
This simple, colorful book is filled with easy-to-understand information about trains.

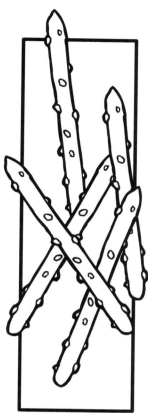

Trains

Let's Sing: Choo-Choo Songs

Choo, Choo, Choo for the Train
(to the tune of "Take Me Out to the Ball Game")

We went down to the station,
We went down by the tracks,
I saw a freight car and engine, too.
I heard the train whistle sound out, "whooo-whooo."

The conductor calls, "All aboard, now,"
And passengers hurry inside.
And it's choo, choo, choo for the train,
While we wave good-bye.

Choo, Choo, Choo!
(to the tune of "Clementine")

At the station, I've been watching,
As the trains go rumbling past.
There are freight trains, with their big cars,
There are speed trains going fast.

But my favorites are the engines,
When they whistle loud and true,
And I wave as they drive by me,
Singing with them, "Choo-choo-choo!"

Other Train Songs:
- "I've Been Working on the Railroad"
- "Down by the Station"

"I'm a Train!"

Airplanes

Introduction

• Let's Read:
Mr. Lunch Takes a Plane Ride by J. Otto Seibold and Vivian Walsh (Viking, 1993).
Mr. Lunch, a dog, is invited to show his bird-chasing skills on television. Before the trip, Mr. Lunch checks the map, packs, and says good-bye to his friends. Since he's a dog, Mr. Lunch must ride in the baggage compartment, where he explores through other people's luggage. Unfortunately, he doesn't remember which objects go into which suitcases.

• Let's Talk:
Before Mr. Lunch travels on an airplane, he prepares for his trip. Have the children discuss preparations they may have made prior to any time they have traveled. (Their travels need not have been on an airplane. Car trips, bus trips, and train trips can all be included.) If there are children who haven't been on a trip, have them tell where they would like to go in the future and why. Let all of the children share their ideal destinations. Then find these places on a map or globe.

• Let's Learn:
Some planes have jet engines. Others use propellers. Some airplanes are large and carry many passengers. Others carry only freight or cargo. Most children have seen airplanes flying overhead, but they may not be aware that some planes can land on water. These planes are called seaplanes and have special landing devices that let them float. People who fly airplanes are called pilots.

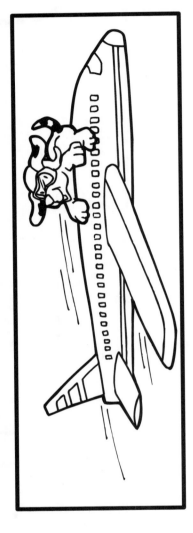

Option:
• Consider stocking your dramatic play corner with small suitcases and old clothes. The children can pack luggage for make-believe trips.

Airplanes

Let's Create: Ticket to Anywhere

What You Need:
Construction paper, scissors, old travel magazines, glue, crayons or markers, maps or globe

What You Do:
1. Have the children look at maps or globes to find a place they would like to visit. Explain that the children can choose a real place, such as Greece, or a type of place, such as an island, a beach, a volcano, a rain forest, and so on.
2. Give each child a sheet of construction paper to use to make a ticket.
3. On the construction paper, the children can paste pictures cut from travel magazines or draw their own pictures of their chosen destinations.
4. When the children have finished drawing pictures, or gluing on pictures, have them dictate the name of the place they'd like to travel to.
5. Post the completed pictures on a "Ticket to Anywhere" bulletin board.

Book Link:
• *Planes* by Anne Rockwell (Dutton, 1985).
This simple book features pictures of planes with propellers, pontoons, jet engines, and more.

Airplanes

Let's Create: Wings to Wear

What You Need:
Wing Patterns (p. 51), scissors, heavy paper, aluminum foil, white labels, marker, glue, hole punch, safety or diaper pins (one per child)

What You Do:
1. Duplicate the Wing Patterns onto heavy paper and cut out. Make enough for each child to have one.
2. Have the children cover the wings with aluminum foil.
3. Write the children's names on the labels, or let the children write their own names on the labels.
4. Have the children put the labels in the center of the wings.
5. Punch two holes in each set of wings. Space the holes so that the pins will fit through.
6. Fasten the wings to the children's clothes using safety pins or diaper pins.
7. The children can pretend that they are pilots while wearing the wings.

Note:
These wings make good name tags during field trips. Or use them as cubby labels or desk labels for Open House nights. The parents will find their children's area based on the names on the wings.

Wing Patterns

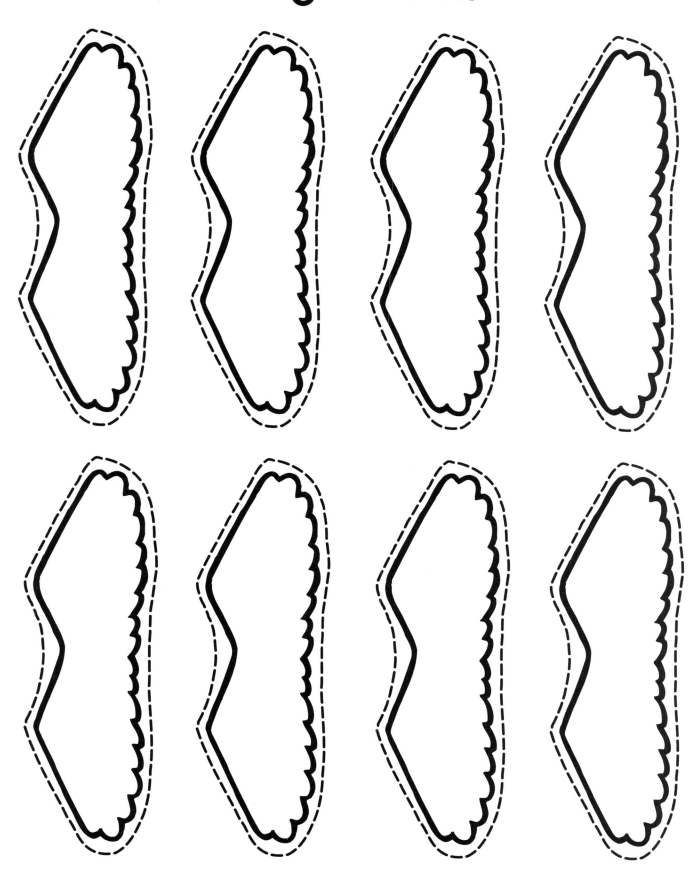

Airplanes

Let's Create: Up, Up, and Away!

Explain that before there were airplanes, people saw the sights in hot air balloons.

What You Need:

Hot Air Balloon (p. 53), tissue paper, glue, shallow tins (for glue), paintbrushes, yarn, scissors, crayons or markers

What You Do:

1. Duplicate a copy of the Hot Air Balloon for each child.
2. Let the children decorate the balloons with scraps of tissue paper. They can paint the scraps in place using glue.
3. Provide pieces of colored yarn for the children to glue onto their pictures in place of the string that holds the balloons to the baskets.
4. Have the children draw pictures of themselves and their friends or family in the baskets of the balloons.
5. Post the finished pictures on a window, where the light will shine through the balloons.

Option:

• Have the parents send photos of their children from home. (Explain that the photographs will be used in an art project and will not be returned in whole condition.) The children can glue their pictures in the basket portions of the balloons.

Hot Air Balloon

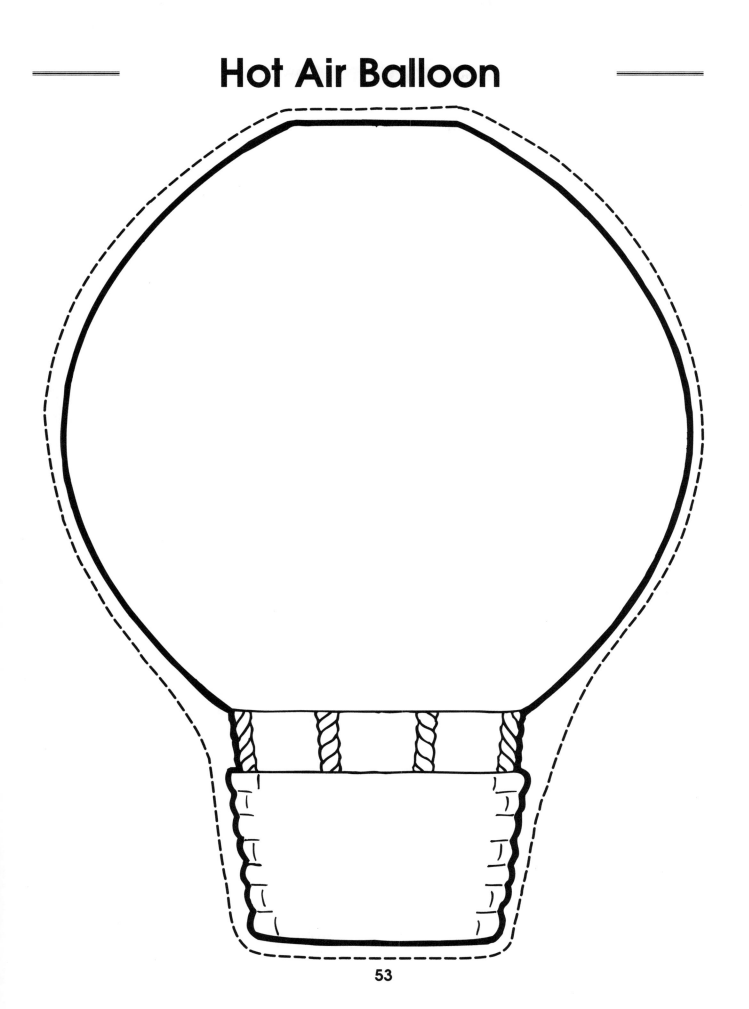

Airplanes

Let's Find Out: Suitcase Sorting

Mr. Lunch causes some problems by putting people's belongings in the wrong suitcases. In this activity, the children try their hand at correctly sorting objects into suitcases.

What You Need:
Suitcase Pattern (p. 55), Clothes Patterns (below), marker, colored construction paper, scissors

What You Do:
1. Duplicate 26 copies of the suitcase. Write a different capital letter of the alphabet on each suitcase.
2. Duplicate the Clothes Patterns onto colored construction paper. Write a different lowercase letter on each pattern.
3. Spread the suitcases on the floor or on a low table.
4. Have the children match the lowercase letters (written on the clothes) with the uppercase letters (on the luggage).
5. Store the suitcases and the lowercase letter shapes in a large envelope. The children can practice sorting during free time.

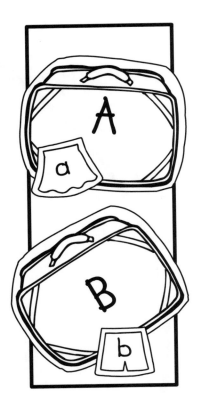

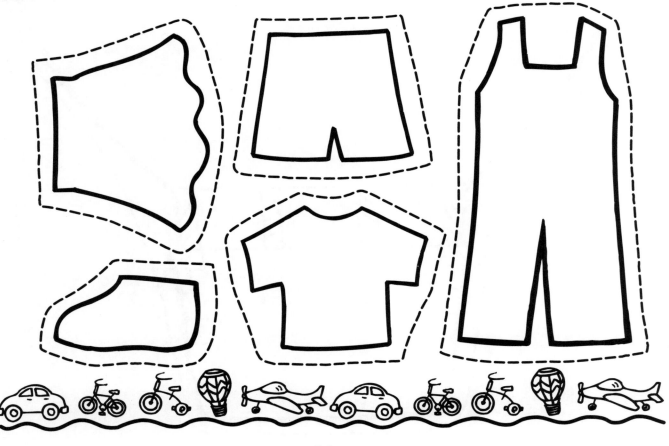

Suitcase Pattern

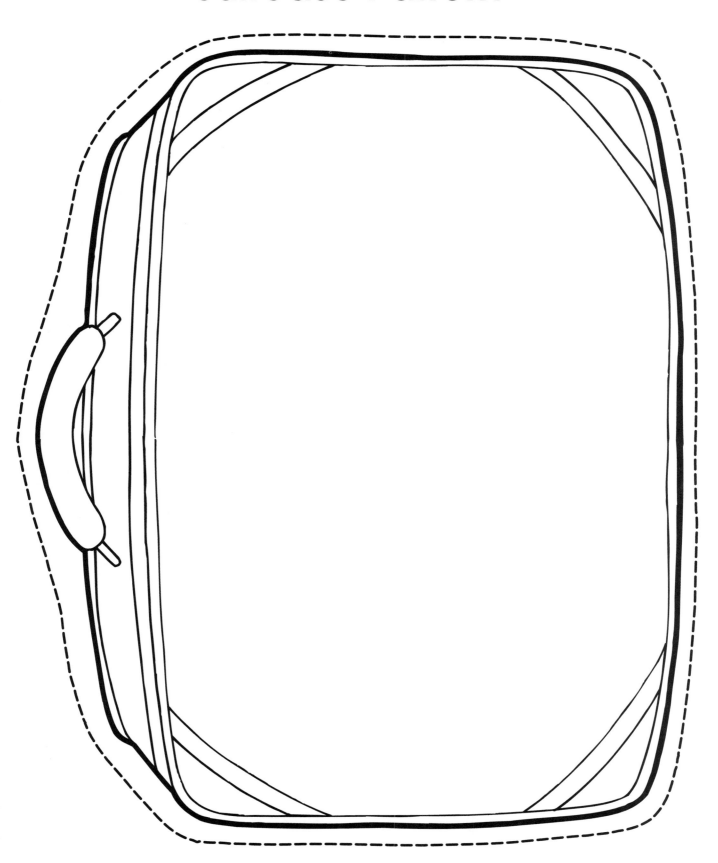

Airplanes

Let's Find Out: Airplane Math

What You Need:
Airplane Patterns (p. 57), Suitcase Patterns (p. 58), scissors

What You Do:
1. Duplicate the airplanes and suitcases. Either make a set for each child, or for each small group of children. (Cut out the patterns, or let the children cut them out.)
2. Have the children work individually or in small groups to match the numeral on the airplanes with the correct suitcases. Check their work. Make sure each child has a chance to match at least one suitcase to one airplane.

Options:
• White-out the numbers and the dots. Write color words on the airplanes and color the suitcases to match. The children will match the colored suitcases with the color words written on the airplanes.
• Duplicate 26 suitcases and airplanes. Write a lowercase letter on each plane and an uppercase letter on each suitcase. The children will match the upper- and lowercase patterns.
• Duplicate enough airplanes for each child to have several. Let the children color the planes and cut them out. Punch a hole in each one and thread through with string. Let the children attach the planes to wire hangers. They can cover the body of the hangers with felt or paper. Hang these airplane mobiles around the room.

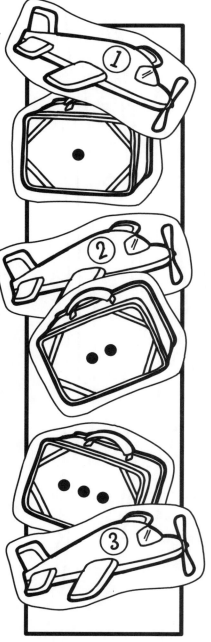

Airplane Patterns

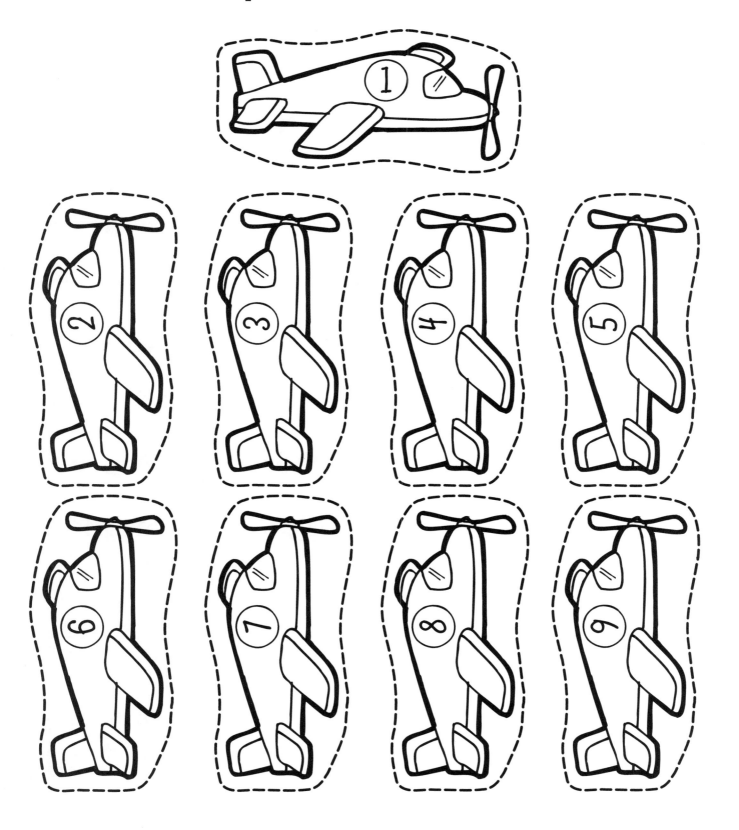

Suitcase Patterns

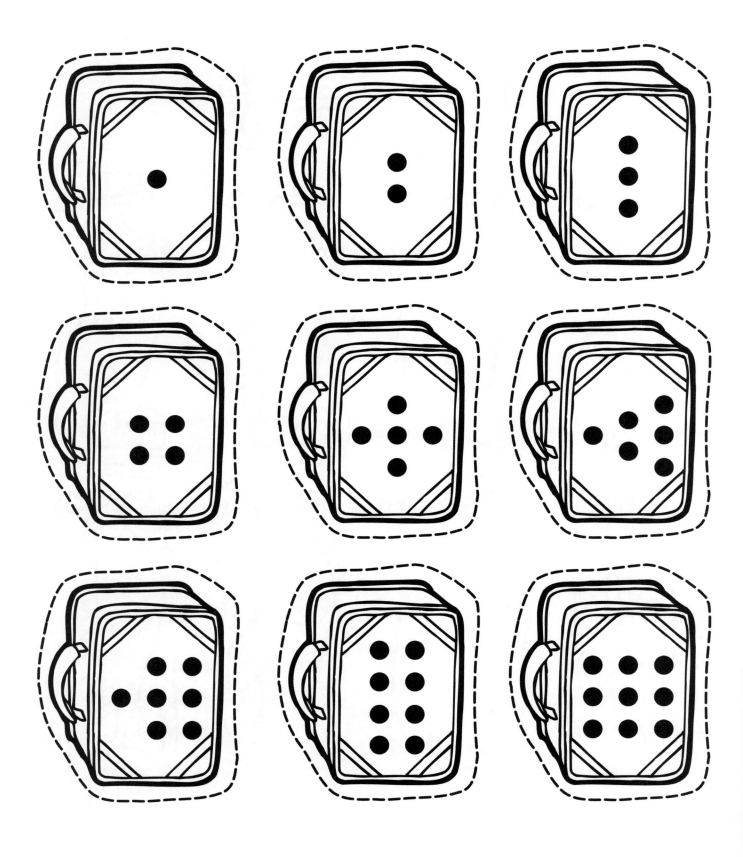

Airplanes

Let's Play: Plane-Centration

This game is played like "Concentration."

What You Need:
Plane-Centration Cards (p. 60), markers or crayons, scissors, clear contact paper or laminator (optional)

What You Do:
1. Duplicate the cards twice, color, and cut out. Laminate or cover with clear contact paper, if desired. Cut out again leaving a thin laminate border to prevent peeling.
2. Demonstrate how to play "Plane-Centration." The children turn all the cards face down. The first child turns two cards over at a time. If the cards match, the child keeps them and takes another turn. If the cards do not match, the child turns them back over and another child takes a turn.

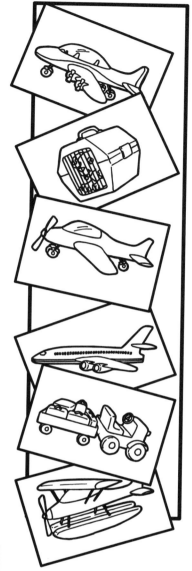

Plane-Centration Cards

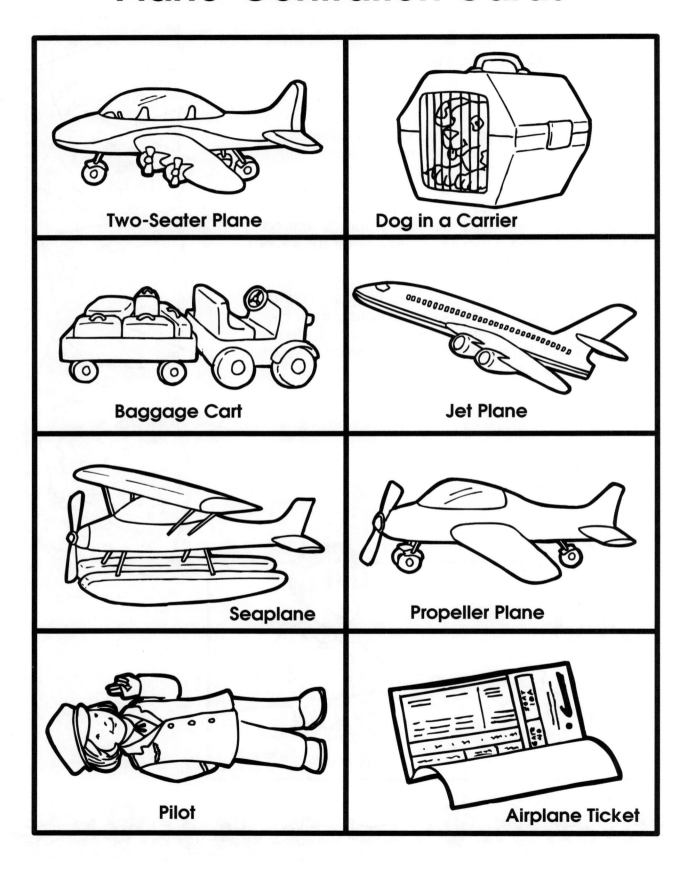

Two-Seater Plane

Dog in a Carrier

Baggage Cart

Jet Plane

Seaplane

Propeller Plane

Pilot

Airplane Ticket

Airplanes

Let's Eat: Airplane Food

Airplane food has a bad reputation. However, the children will enjoy eating food off of compartment-style plates while pretending to be in an airplane.

What You Need:

Compartment-style paper plates (the type that has dividers to separate the food), bite-size snacks (such as celery sticks, carrot sticks, cheese cubes, apple slices, orange slices)

What You Do:

1. Set up the room so that the desks or chairs are in rows, the way they would be on a plane.
2. Arrange the snacks on the plates so that there is a different type of food in each compartment.
3. Have most of the children sit in their "plane seats," while one or two volunteers serve the snacks by walking down the aisle between the chairs or desks.
4. The children can use any leftover paper plates in their dramatic play about airplanes.

Airplanes

Let's Sing: Flying Song

Up, Up in an Airplane
(to the tune of "On Top of Old Smokey")

Up, up in an airplane,
So high in the sky,
I looked out the window,
And waved down good-bye.

We flew above cities,
With trains, cars, and trucks,
We flew above farmyards,
With cows, pigs, and ducks.

And when the plane landed,
We saw all our friends,
Then climbed on an airplane,
And flew home again.

Let's Learn: Mother Goose Rhyme

What's the news of the day,
Good neighbor, I pray?
They say a balloon
Has gone up to the moon!

"I'm an Airplane!"

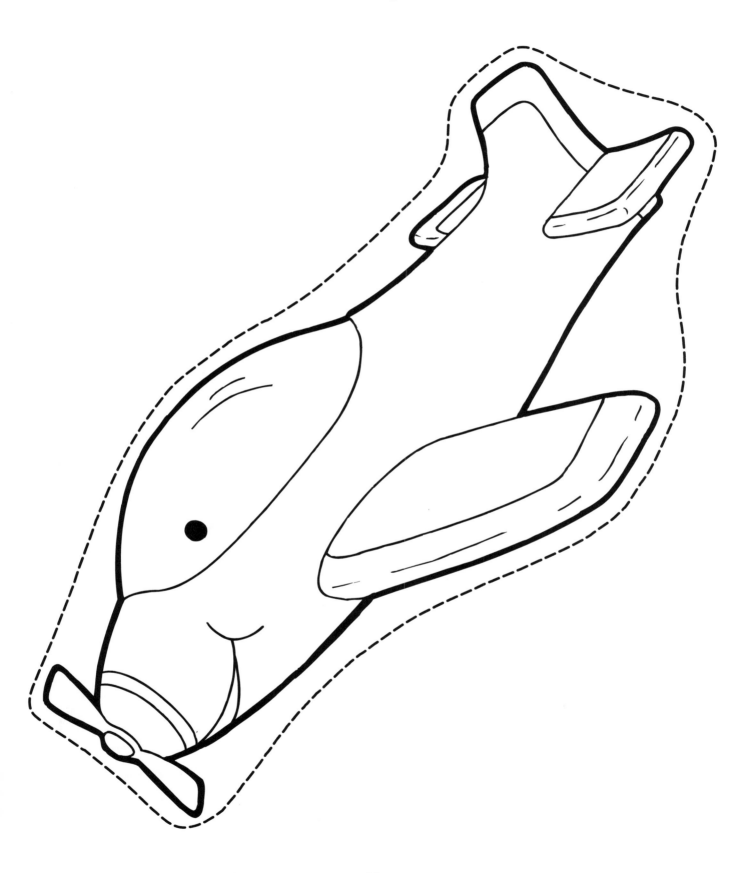

"I'm a Helicopter!"

Bikes & Trikes

Introduction

• Let's Read:
Curious George Rides a Bike by H. A. Rey (Houghton Mifflin, 1952).
When the man with the yellow hat gives George a bike, he goes exploring. First, he helps the paperboy with his route. Then he makes newspaper boats, which he sails in the river. Finally, George helps catch a baby bear! This story includes instructions for making a boat from newspaper.

• Let's Talk:
Curious George becomes part of a traveling animal show for one night only. Let the children share times that they have seen animals—perhaps in a zoo or wild animal park, or in a circus, or on television or in the movies. Let each child share his or her favorite creature.

In order to bring people's attention to the runaway bear, Curious George blows a bugle. Discuss ways that the children could get attention if they needed help. They might blow a whistle, or shout, or ask a police officer or teacher for assistance. Brainstorm different ways that the children could use to get help if they needed it.

• Let's Learn:
Cycles come in many forms. There are three-wheeled tricycles, two-wheeled bicycles, and one-wheeled unicycles. There are bicycles called tandems made for two riders, and even bicycles called triplettes and quadruplettes made for three and four riders. Bicycles were invented more than 200 years ago. Some early bicycles, called "ordinaries," had very large front wheels and small rear wheels. Tricycles, invented about 100 years ago, were safer rides than the ordinaries.

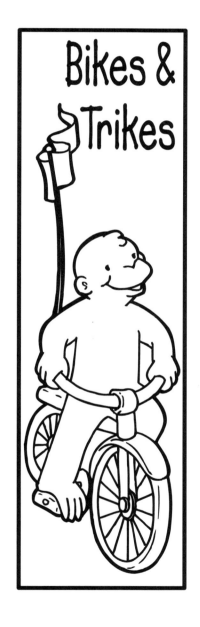

Bikes & Trikes

Let's Create: What's in the Box?

Curious George is a very curious monkey. In *Curious George Rides a Bike*, George rides away from home because he is curious, he visits the river because he is curious, and he feeds an ostrich his bugle because he is curious.

What You Need:
Construction paper, crayons or markers, scissors, box with a lid (a shoe box would work well)

What You Do:
1. Discuss how curious George is in the story. Have the children try to think of a time when they were curious. Let them share their memories of their "curious" experiences.
2. Show the children the box, and ask them to imagine what might be inside it. Explain that there is no right answer.
3. Give each child a piece of construction paper. Have the children draw a picture of what they think might be in the box. Then, have the children cut out their pictures.
4. Gather up all of the pictures and put them in the box.
5. Have the children sit in a circle. One at a time, take their pictures out of the box and show them to the class.
6. Discuss the fact that the children imagined that different things might be in the box.

Book Links:
• *How Many Bugs in a Box?* by David A. Carter (Little Simon, 1988) and *More Bugs in Boxes* by David A. Carter (Little Simon, 1990).

Bikes & Trikes

Let's Find Out: One, Two, Three

In this activity, the children will learn the meaning of the prefixes uni-, bi-, and tri-.

What You Need:

Cycle Patterns (p. 68), small circular plastic lids (ask parents to collect these for you), construction paper, scissors

What You Do:

1. Duplicate the Cycle Patterns. Make one copy for each child.
2. Explain that the word unicycle means one wheel, the word bicycle means two wheels and the word tricycle means three wheels.
3. Give each child a copy of the Cycle Patterns. Have the children name the unicycle, bicycle, and tricycle.
4. Have the children make their own cycles. They can choose to make unicycles, bicycles, or tricycles. The children can glue the lids to the construction paper for the wheels. Or they can trace the lids onto the paper. Then they can draw the rest of the cycles. They can add pictures of themselves riding their creations.
5. Post the completed pictures on a "One, Two, Three" bulletin board.

Option:

• Have the children make up cycle creations with more than three wheels. They can name their creations. Have them count the number of wheels on their paper and write that number next to the cycles.

Cycle Patterns

Bikes & Trikes

Let's Find Out: Pedals and Petals

What You Need:
Chalk, paper, crayons or markers

What You Do:
1. Discuss the words pedal and petal. Write both words on the board and sound them out. Have the children try to guess what the different words mean.
2. Brainstorm with the class other words that sound the same but mean different things. Some words have the same spelling but mean different things.
3. Have the children draw pictures of a bicycle with "petals" for "pedals." Or let them illustrate any other funny sound-alike words.

Similar sounding words:
- ate, eight
- pear, pair, pare
- red, read
- sea, see
- saw (to cut with), saw (past tense of "see")
- hangar, hanger

Option:
- Read either of the books from the book links before doing this activity. The children can recreate pictures from these books if they'd like.

Book Links:
- *A Chocolate Moose for Dinner* by Fred Gwynne (Turtleback, 1988).
- *The King Who Rained* by Fred Gwynne (Aladdin, 1988).

Bikes & Trikes

Let's Find Out: Helmets and Hard Hats
A bicycle chapter is the perfect time to talk about bicycle safety.

What You Need:
Workers (p. 71), Safety Devices (p. 72), crayons or markers, scissors, envelopes

What You Do:
1. Explain that different types of jobs have different safety precautions. Have the children brainstorm safety devices that go with different occupations or hobbies.
2. Duplicate the Workers and Safety Devices Patterns. Make one set for every two children. Have the children work together to match the people with their safety gear.
3. The children can color the sets when they're finished matching people with their gear.
4. Have the children store the patterns in envelopes when they're finished.

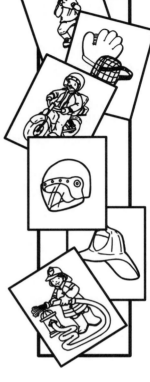

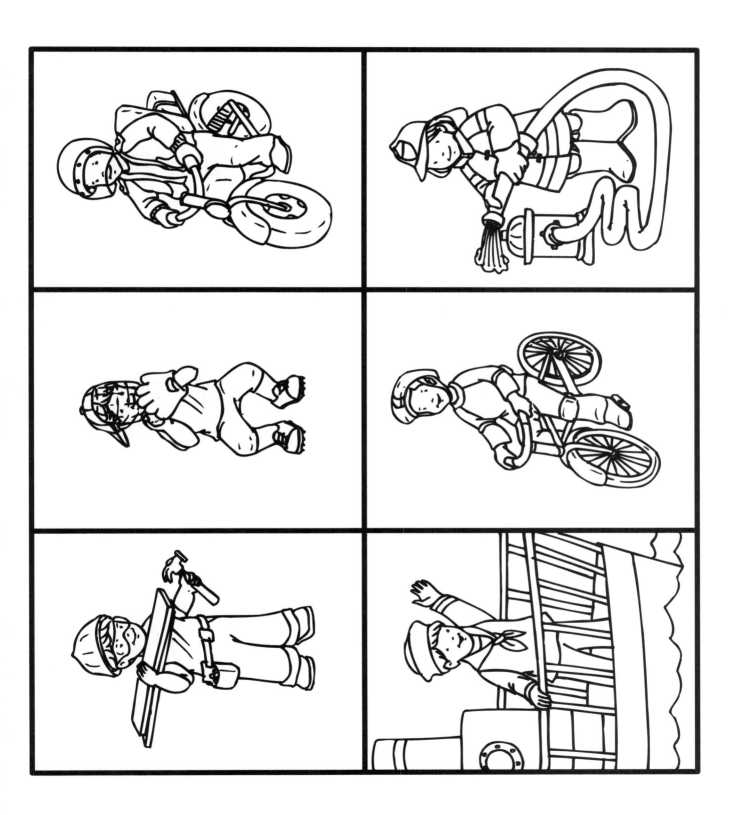

Safety Devices

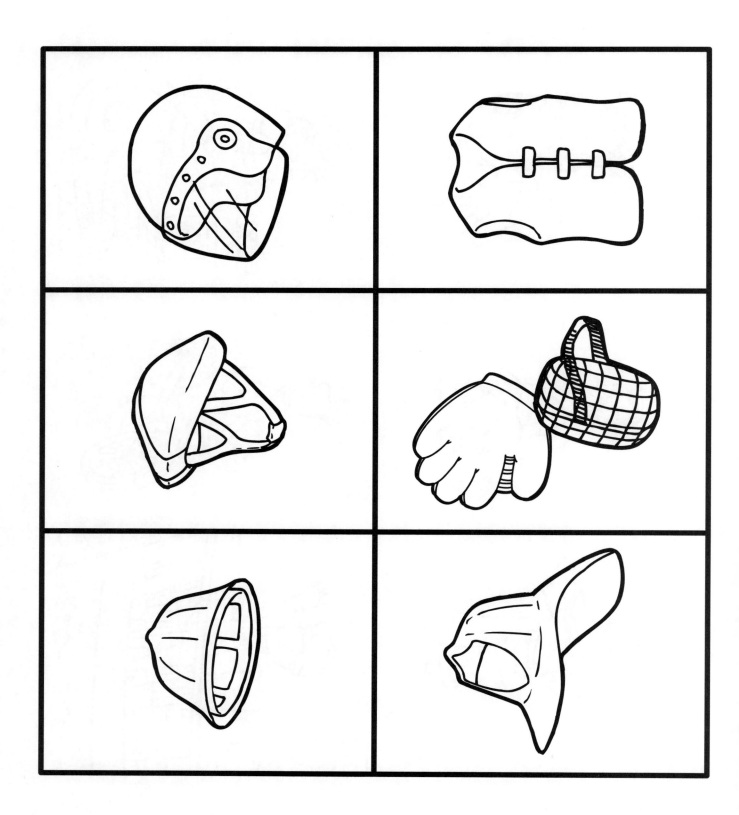

Bikes & Trikes

Let's Play: Bicycle Race

What You Need:
Markers and Spinner (p. 74), Game Board pattern (p. 75), crayons or markers, clear contact paper (or laminating machine), scissors, hole punch, brad

What You Do:
1. Duplicate the Game Board pattern, color, and cover with contact paper. (Or use a laminating machine.)
2. Duplicate the Markers and Spinner, cut out, color, cover with clear contact paper, and cut out again. (Leave a thin laminate border to help prevent peeling.)
3. Punch a hole in the center of the spinner, and attach the arrow using the brad.
4. Explain the game to the children. Three players may play at a time. The children are bicycle riders traveling through the park. Each one is trying to get to the end of the park first. The first child to land at the spot marked "finish" is the winner.

Markers & Spinner

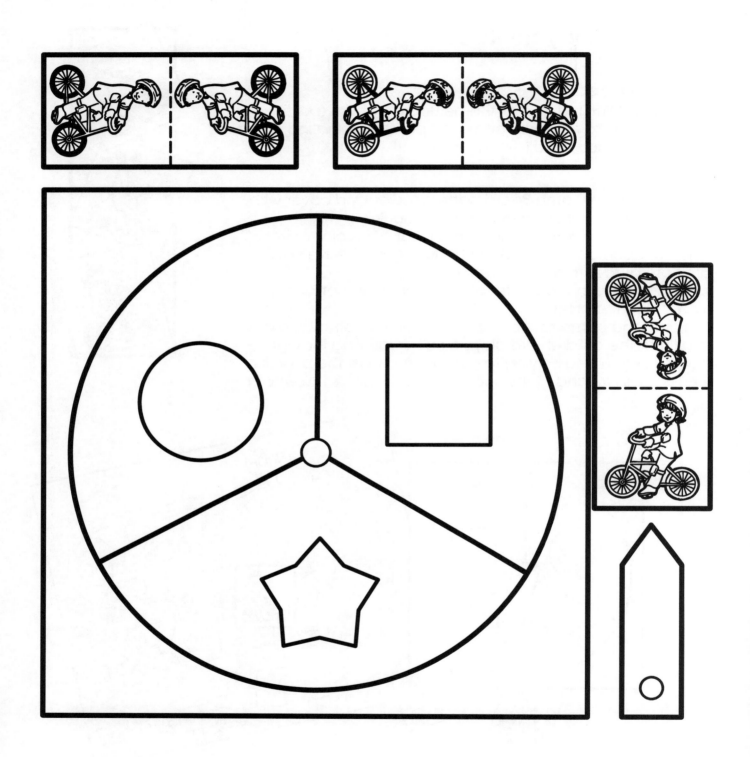

Game Board

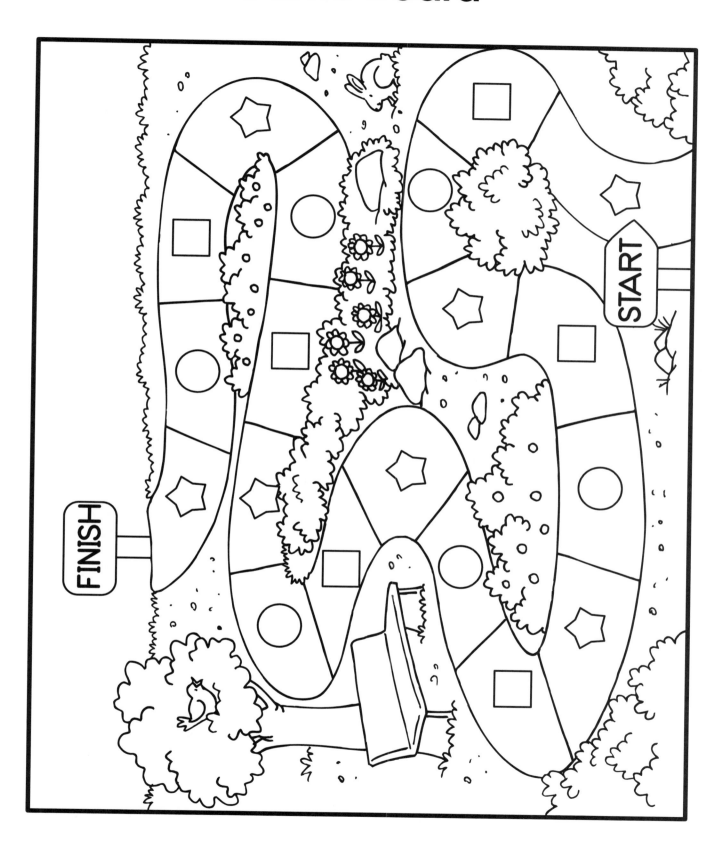

Bikes & Trikes

Let's Sing: Bicycle Songs

"I Learned to Ride a Bike"
(to the tune of "The Farmer in the Dell")

I learned to ride a bike.
I learned to ride a bike.
Hi-ho-the-derry-oh,
I learned to ride a bike!

"Ride, Ride, Ride Your Bike"
(to the tune of "Row, Row, Row Your Boat")

Ride, ride, ride your bike,
Ride from home to school,
Don't forget, don't forget, don't forget, don't forget,
Helmets are the rule!

"A Bicycle Is Made with Two Wheels"
(to the tune of "My Bonnie Lies Over the Ocean")

A bicycle is made with two wheels.
A tricycle is made with three.
A tandem is built for two riders.
But my bike is fine for just me, just me.
I like to ride on my bicycle built for just me, just me.
I like to ride on my bicycle built just for me.

"We're Cycles!"

Storybook Resources

Airplanes:
• *I Fly* by Anne Rockwell, illustrated by Annette Cable (Crown, 1997).
This book follows a child on an airplane ride.
• *Richard Scarry's Great Big Air Book* by Richard Scarry (Random House, 1971).
This fun, fact-filled book explains not only how airplanes fly but also how birds fly.

Automobiles
• *Beep! Beep!* by Anne Miranda, illustrated by David Murphy (Turtle, 1999).
A child pretends to be different vehicles and the noises that they make. Also by the author and illustrator, *Vroom, Chugga, Vroom-Vroom* (Turtle, 1998).
• *Cars* by Anne Rockwell (Dutton, 1984).
A very simple book about cars and where they drive.
• *Miss Spider's New Car* by David Kirk (Scholastic, 1997).
This installment in the Miss Spider series is as beautifully illustrated as the rest.

Bicycles:
• *Mrs. Armitage on Wheels* by Quentin Blake (Knopf, 1987).
Mrs. Armitage decides that the bell on her bike isn't loud enough, so she buys three horns.

Cable Cars:
• *Maybelle the Cable Car* by Virginia Lee Burton (Houghton Mifflin, 1952).

School Buses:
• *Albert's Field Trip* by Leslie Tryon (Atheneum, 1993).
Albert the duck plans a field trip to Georgie and Gracie's Apple Farm. The children ride a big, yellow school bus to get to the farm.
• *The Magic School Bus: Lost in the Solar System* by Joanna Cole, illustrated by Bruce Degen (Scholastic, 1990).
Ms. Frizzle's class takes a wild ride through space on a magic school bus. They visit planets, the sun, the moon, and the asteroid belt. This series features many other magic journeys.

Storybook Resources

Taxis:
• *The Adventures of Taxi Dog* by Debra and
Sal Barracca (Dial, 1990).
A Reading Rainbow book and a Public Television
Storytime Book.
• *Daisy's Taxi* by Ruth Young, illustrated by Marcia Sewall
(Orchard, 1991).
Daisy's taxi isn't a normal taxi. It's a boat that she rows from
the mainland to the island every day.
• *The Taxi That Hurried* by Lucy Sprague Mitchell, Irma
Simonton Black, and Jessie Stanton, illustrated by Tibor
Gergely (Golden, 1946).

Trains:
• *All Aboard ABC* by Doug Magger and Robert Newman
(Dutton, 1990).
• *The Caboose Who Got Loose* by Bill Peet
(Houghton Mifflin, 1971).
Katy Caboose doesn't like being the last car on the train.
• *John Henry* by Julius Lester and Jerry Pinkney (Dial, 1994).
This is a Caldecott Honor Book.
• *The Polar Express* by Chris Van Allsburg
(Houghton Mifflin, 1985).
This classic is a perfect book to read during the winter
holidays.
• *Puzzle Train* by Susannah Leigh (EDC, 1995).
• *The Train to Timbuctoo* by Margaret Wise Brown
(Golden Books, 1999).
• *Trains* by Angela Royston (Aladdin, 1992).

Nonfiction Resources

Airplanes:
- *Going on an Airplane* by Fred Rogers, photographs by Jim Judkis (Putnam, 1989).
- *Your First Airplane Trip* by Pat and Joel Ross, illustrated by Lynn Wheeling (Lothrop, 1981).

Automobiles:
- *Cars and How They Work* by Gordon Cruikshank, illustrated by Alan Austin (Dorling Kindersley, 1992).
This is a fact-filled book that children will enjoy paging through.
- *Cars and Trucks* by Philip Steele (Crestwood House, 1991).
This book is filled with pictures and facts to share with the children. Pick and choose facts that the children will enjoy and understand.

Bicycles:
- *Bicycle Book* by Gail Gibbons (Holiday House, 1995).
- *The Bicycle & How It Works* by David Inglis Urquhart (Henry Z. Walck, 1972).
This book is too advanced to read to the children, but it contains interesting facts to share.

Variety of Transportation:
- *On the Go* by Ann Morris, photographs by Ken Heyman (Lothrop, 1990).
This book focuses on some of the many different means of transportation around the world, including camels, oxen, buses, trolleys, and monorails.
- *Things that Go* by Anne Rockwell (Dutton, 1986).
This book is divided into sections, including things that go on the road, in the air, on water, and more.